I'M GOING TO BE A
PILOT!

T0191349

BY MICHOU FRANCO

Gareth Stevens
PUBLISHING

Please visit our website, www.garethstevens.com. For a free color catalog of all our high-quality books, call toll free 1-800-542-2595 or fax 1-877-542-2596.

Library of Congress Cataloging-in-Publication Data

Names: Franco, Michou, author.
Title: I'm going to be a pilot! / Michou Franco.
Description: Buffalo, NY : Gareth Stevens Publishing, [2025] | Series:
    That's the job for me! | Includes bibliographical references and index.
Identifiers: LCCN 2023037231 (print) | LCCN 2023037232 (ebook) | ISBN
    9781538293324 (library binding) | ISBN 9781538293317 (paperback) | ISBN
    9781538293331 (ebook)
Subjects: LCSH: Airplanes–Piloting–Vocational guidance–Juvenile
    literature. | Aeronautics–Vocational guidance–Juvenile literature.
Classification: LCC TL561 .F73 2025 (print) | LCC TL561 (ebook) | DDC
    629.132/52023–dc23/eng/20230824
LC record available at https://lccn.loc.gov/2023037231
LC ebook record available at https://lccn.loc.gov/2023037232

Published in 2025 by
Gareth Stevens Publishing
2544 Clinton Street
Buffalo, NY 14224

Copyright © 2025 Gareth Stevens Publishing

Designer: Claire Zimmermann
Editor: Therese Shea

Photo credits: Cover, pp. 1, 7 ravipat/Shutterstock.com; Series Art (background) Salmanalfa/Shutterstock.com; p. 5 MNStudio/Shutterstock.com; p. 7 CarlosBarquero/Shutterstock.com; p. 9 Stokkete/Shutterstock.com; p. 11 Ververidis Vasilis/Shutterstock.com; p. 13 Toni. M/Shutterstock.com; p. 15 Demkat/Shutterstock.com; p. 17 Olga Steckel/ Shutterstock.com; p. 19 palawat744/Shutterstock.com; p. 21 Yuganov Konstantin/Shutterstock.com.

Printed in the United States of America

Some of the images in this book illustrate individuals who are models. The depictions do not imply actual situations or events.

CPSIA compliance information: Batch #CS25GS: For further information contact Gareth Stevens, New York, New York at 1-800-542-2595.

Find us on

CONTENTS

Boldface words appear in the glossary.

Becoming a Pilot

I love flying. I love how the world looks from high in the sky. Everything looks so tiny! And I really love to travel. I'm going to be a pilot. A pilot is the person who flies an aircraft, such as an airplane or **helicopter**.

License to Fly

First, I need to decide what kind of pilot I want to be! Different pilots need different **licenses**. All pilots take classes on the ground and in the air. They also have to pass tests on the ground and in the air. Helicopter pilots take different classes and tests than airplane pilots.

Kinds of Pilots

Some people have a **private** pilot license. They can get this license after 40 hours of flying practice or more. A private pilot license means these pilots can fly for fun. But they can't fly as a job.

More classes and training can lead to a **commercial** pilot license. Commercial pilots can get jobs flying people and cargo, or goods. They can take **tourists** on rides. They can fly firefighting airplanes too! These planes spray water on fires.

Some commercial pilots do even more training to get an airline pilot license. An airline is a company that carries passengers, or riders, and cargo using different **routes**. In the United States, a pilot needs to fly 1,500 hours before they can become an airline pilot!

13

Where to Learn

Some people go to flight schools to get the license they want. Others go to **college** to study **aviation**. There, they learn a lot about how aircraft work. Some people learn to become pilots in the military, or armed forces.

14

Military Pilots

The U.S. Air Force, Navy, Army, and Marines have flight training. Military pilots are needed to transport, or carry, soldiers and gear. They have other **missions** in wars. The U.S. Navy's Blue Angels show off their skills by doing **stunts** in the air!

Pilot and Copilot

On airline flights, the pilot in command is in charge of the flight. The copilot is second in command and helps with many flight duties. Before, during, and after each flight, both pilots check the plane's systems and controls to make sure everything is working well.

Ready for Takeoff!

Pilots need other skills too. They must **communicate** well with passengers and **air traffic control**. They also need to stay calm in danger. They may need to act quickly to save lives. I can't wait to be a pilot!

GLOSSARY

air traffic control: The system that directs movements of aircraft. Ground workers communicate with pilots by radio.

aviation: The act, practice, or science of flying aircraft.

college: A school after high school.

commercial: Having to do with the buying and selling of goods and services.

communicate: To share ideas through sounds and motions.

helicopter: An aircraft without wings that uses fast-moving blades to move.

license: A paper that allows someone to do something.

mission: A task or job a group must perform.

private: Having to do with one person, not the public.

route: A course or path that people travel.

stunt: A dangerous action done to entertain people.

tourist: Someone who travels to visit a place.

FOR MORE INFORMATION

BOOKS

Bender, Douglas. *Pilot*. New York, NY: Crabtree Publishing, 2023.

Culliford, Amy. *Someday I Could Bee a Pilot!* New York, NY: Crabtree Publishing Company, 2022.

WEBSITES

Parts of a Plane
www.grc.nasa.gov/www/k-12/UEET/StudentSite/airplanes.html
NASA explains the parts of a plane and how it takes flight.

Pilot
kids.britannica.com/kids/article/pilot/353629
Read more about pilot skills and find out about the world's youngest pilot.

INDEX